Disappearing – How to start a new life

How to disappear completely, how to create a new identity, and how to start over

By Robert Anderson

Disclaimer

Every attempt has been made to verify the information within this book, author assumes no responsibility for errors, omissions, or opposite opinions. This book is for informational purposes only and the writing is the opinion of the author only. This publication should not be construed as legal advice, tax advice, business advice, or any other advice. Reader assumes responsibility to verify all information and the legal responsibility for using the information.

Reader should seek any professional for advice regarding his or her personal situation from legal experts, tax experts, government entities, or others that may provide expert guidance and information. Author assumes no accountability or responsibility for anything the reader uses from this publication that can be construed as illegal, unethical, immoral, or otherwise. It is up to the reader to adhere to all laws and regulations by any government or entity in all countries and jurisdictions. Any perceived slight to any individual or entity is purely coincidental and not intentional.

Table of Contents

4

Introduction

Many people think about the idea and possibility of starting a new life and having a fresh start. Few have the testicular fortitude to do it because they don't know what to do and are scared to try. If you are contemplating it, you can do it with the proper resources, planning, and time.

People today love their comfort zones and do not like change. It's the classic syndrome of whether you are sad and stressed enough to get out of your situation, or if you are just contempt enough to stay in your mundane life because it "might" get better. This is why so many choose suicide today rather than making a change. They see no other way out. Guess what? You are holding the way out in your hand.

Throughout history, the human experience has been to be on the go and nomadic. In the last century, American culture has deemed that people should locate to one place and stay there until the day they die. Families want to set roots in communities, and this has worked for the last couple generations. Many in the younger generations today want to move and be mobile, there are a lot that have done away with what culture deems "normal" and are now living mobile lives in RVs or in tiny homes, or are moving frequently so that they can be on the go and not have to be tied to one location. This is a great thing for people like you that want to disappear because moving around and not having the socially accepted normal life is okay in many people's eyes.

Relationships between employers and employees has also changed in the last 40 years, if you look through social profiles on LinkedIn or at resumes of most people, they are at a place of employment for a while then move on. This also bodes well for the disappearing act because people don't question now why you have not stayed at a job for more than a couple years and have multiple jobs on your resume.

This is a balancing act that you must be good at though because as a race, the humans are wanting to have so much verifiable information and details of our lives that in years past was not important. Everything we do now in society is recorded and people want to know everything about everyone. You cannot walk into a gas station now without them offering you a membership card that requires your name, address, telephone number, and email address. Information gathering has gotten out of control, and people mindlessly give it out to whomever asks now.

My writing style is straight forward and to the point, as the reason for my writing is to get all the facts about a subject from many areas by research and experience, package it up in an understandable and logical format, and present it to people like you so that you know all the facts and steps to accomplish what you want to accomplish. Writing for understanding has been a passion of mine for a long time. I have packaged it up in a clear way, this is the best way I can present it.

The information contained herein will give you as much information as I know at the present time, and will teach you how to disappear. So, I cut through the bullshit, and give you what you need. In my research I read so many things that people write that ramble on and on in mindless dribble that I want to save you from that pain. Many also do not follow a straight path from where you are to where you want to go, rather jumble everything into a book that leaves you wondering what to do and in what order. Use the techniques and tactics provided here and change your life.

This book is a comprehensive how to guide to disappearing, but it is not all the information you will need. Your ability to research and find all the information will help you to be successful. While I tried to encompass everything and make this a guide that could get you from where you are now to where you want to be, I'm sure I missed some things. If you have any questions that are not answered here or you have any suggestions as to what can be added to future renditions, let me know. At the end of the book is information on how to ask me questions or make suggestions. I suggest you read the whole book before you come up with these as the answers may be within these pages.

It will also not discuss illegal ways of disappearing because this is not something I think should be done. If you need to illegally disappear, then there are many other resources to look up to do so. Many of the things in this book will help you ven if you are disappearing illegally, just not outline the means to get fake documents to create a fake identification. If ou read through this book and find you do not have to illegally create your new identity, kudos to you.

nother thing to note is this book assumes you have time to plan and put actions into place that are going to help get ou off the radar in your old life, plan your escape, and set you up to be successful in your new life, so you may read ome things and tell yourself that you can't do that. If you can't that is fine, just pull out the things you can do and read n. Everyone's situation is different when it comes to time, money, and other resources to disappear and some of what in here you are not able to do. If you must get out tomorrow, take what you can (including a copy of this book) to get a safe place, then start rebuilding from there. Remember though, the time and effort you put into preparing will make our escape much easier to accomplish, and starting your new life easier.

also suggest that you read through the book a couple times, the first one just to start getting the concepts in your head. hen you should go through the book page by page to start formulating your plan and do the activities necessary to ccessfully disappear. You should also have a highlighter in hand or pen and paper to write down the steps that apply o you so that you can create a checklist of things you need to take care of in your planning for your new life and ccessfully setting up your new life.

ou may read through this book too and be overwhelmed by the amount of information you have to think about and nd out to successfully disappear, along with all the planning, preparation, and things you must do to successfully isappear. This was done on purpose so that you understand the magnitude of what you are getting ready to do. If it ere easy, everyone would be doing it. Only those truly committed to doing what has to be done will read this whole ook and do all the steps and actions needed to successfully disappear. This notion you have to vanish is not for the faint f heart, because this is the biggest risk you will ever take in your life.

ne other thing, if you found this book on your home computer by searching the Internet from your home, the first commendation I have is to make it the last thing you look up about disappearing and doing research into your new life n your home computer, Kindle, smart phone, or tablet. It leaves trails. If someone gets ahold of the device and earches it, they will find any information you looked up, saved, or even deleted because it will be there. This can lead to ou being caught in your new identity. Read this book and find out how to make it so no one finds the information you eek.

Why people decide to start over

I don't know why you decided to get this book, there are many different reasons why people decide they have had enough of their current life and want a do-over and a fresh start to things. Whatever your reason is, before you look into the mechanics of it all, you must look at the emotional side of it. Leaving your current life, even if you do not have a large family and a big group of friends will still impact the people that are in your life now because to them you may as well be dead. You must cut all ties to these people to successfully stay hidden. This will impact you emotionally because at some point you are going to feel lonely and be alone, and one thought that will pop into your head is to get in touch with them to comfort your own heart. This is one of the easiest ways to get caught.

The people you leave will also be hurt by your decision to sneak off into your new life because you are not telling them where you are going, why you left, and how they could have done something different to prevent you from going. Your children, if you have any, may be scarred for life because of your disappearance, and if you have a significant other that thinks everything is going great to find you one day disappeared, he or she will be devastated. Likewise, your family, friends, acquaintances, and co-workers will also be affected by your leaving.

You definitely can replace people in your life after you leave, although it will take time and the rest of your life will be half-truths and even lies to do what you are embarking on. It must be this way to keep hidden from what you left. Getting into a new relationship will also be fraught with lies because you must never reveal your true self or it will unravel your new self.

I just binged watched the series Dexter on Netflix and this was a perfect example of the difficulties of hiding your true self to others and in the end, he had to fake his own death then ended up a nobody at a logging camp in his new life. Watch this series and see the difficulty of not being able to be your true self to everyone in your life and around you. I hope you are not a mass-serial killer wanting to escape like Dexter was, you have your own reasons though.

What is your deep reason and desire to want to walk away from your life? Think about it really hard and long before you make a move. Knowing the real reason that you are disappearing will help you in a couple of ways. It will tell you how deep under you must go, and have a better idea of who will be looking for you when you do. It will also determine how far away you need to get from where your old life was. Minimum should be 150 miles and at least one state.

The biggest group of people that disappear and start a new life are middle-aged men with Gauguin Syndrome. These are men that have gotten half way through their lives and realized that it turned out nothing like they planned, they are unhappy and depressed, that feel in their current situation they cannot achieve their dreams and goals as they envisioned them in younger years. Leaving for a new start sounds refreshing.

There are the criminal types that are running away from bad life choices to have an opportunity to start over without having to look over their shoulder to see if the police, mob members, cult members, or gang members are stalking them. These can be the most difficult people to hide because many have a criminal record and will always be in a law enforcement database and if they unluckily get pulled over and checked by a cop the gig is up.

Some people will have to get away because of people in their lives that are wreaking havoc on them and escaping is their only option. If someone has a stalker that won't give up, their lives could be in danger because many stalkers become so psychopathic that they eventually try to kill the victim of their stalking. Many people in a bad marriage that include physical or mental abuse want to get away from it without that person knowing where they are going.

Senior citizens are out there too that are not making enough income with their Social Security checks and retirement money that they need another identity to hide extra income that will not affect their retirement accounts and amounts. Let's say you got with a company or business partner and things went bad between you or with the money and you had to get away to protect yourself financially or from physical harm. Changing your identity could help you with that.

Another group of people that may choose to get a new identity are those that have come into a financial windfall. Some people may have hit the lottery, while others may have gotten a big settlement or money from an estate. Many times, when people get a large sum of money, everyone and their brother comes knocking on the door for handouts. This could be family, friends, charitable organizations, or any other person and the person that got the money becomes a target for those people. It is not that these people are necessarily bad people, but it can be overwhelming for those that are put in that position.

A few people are out there that want to disappear for true privacy. In the last couple of decades, privacy has been invaded at an exceptional rate in many different ways. The Internet has propagated that in ways many people do not understand. First, check out Google that serves as a platform to scour the Internet for any place online that has your information on websites and social media sites. Then there are the websites that have collected all the public and private information on you that they can get their hands on and put it into a nice little package with a bow for anyone wanting to spend $19.95 for the information.

Then there are the myths (that may be true) that organizations and hackers can watch you through your computer camera and I have even heard of televisions being able to watch people. Whether this is true or not, it could be. Cameras are almost normal now in public, from ATMs to businesses, and public cameras are all over the place for the law to keep an eye on the citizens.

Personal debt is another reason people choose to escape their current life, when bankruptcy is not an option. Having a large tax debt is another issue some are dealing with. Student debt has skyrocketed in the last decade, and people have been thrown into financial turmoil because of the economy and joblessness and underemployment in the country.

People have lost their homes, their cars, and their possessions because of the financial debacle we went through. If you are escaping your debtors, they will try to find you, and they can be a pain in the ass. Eventually that debt will disappear, it may take up to 20 years though. If you are running from taxes or government backed student loans, they will never go away and you will always be hiding.

Then there are those that in my mind truly deserve the Darwin Award. These are people that have financially screwed their lives up and the only option they see is to leave their current life to fake their deaths (Pseudocide) to try to gain the insurance money somehow to start a new life.

Maybe you are reading this solely because you want to see what your options are...

One thing to keep in mind when you decide to run is the people that will come looking for you after you are gone. They will. This is important because depending on their level will depend on how far and how long they can look for you. If you are not happy with life and want a fresh start, have no debt and your bills are paid off, you have cash to get away and are single with no kids you will find it rather easy to walk away because you don't owe anyone anything and have little that attaches you to others.

On the other hand, if you are a criminal that just got out of jail and is on parole, owe a lot of money to others, and have a few kids that you owe child support on, you have many interested in finding you. If you are the Darwin example I gave above and you fake your death for the insurance money, you better be damn good at what you are getting ready to do. Most of you will fall somewhere in between these two scenarios, and should think about who would come looking for you if you disappear.

When it comes to individuals looking for you, they typically have limited resources to track you down. Included could be fees for online searches, private investigators, traveling, and other stuff that at some point in the future they will exhaust their funds for and give up. If it is a business that is looking for you, they can access a little more time and funds in tracking you down because they have more resources. When it comes to any government agency, and to an extent an insurance agency, you better leave the country under an assumed identity and move frequently to keep from being found.

In the United States of America, it is completely legal for an adult to leave, unannounced, without telling anyone where you are going to. You can; however, be held legally liable for how you disappear if you make it appear that you faked your own death. It does not have to be for reasons of collecting insurance money like the Darwin above. The government, namely the police departments will send out search teams to look for you and this costs money. Unless you leave false trails to let people know you left on your own without telling them where you went, you can get into trouble.

As I said earlier, on its own level of stupidity, faking your own death to try and collect insurance money is one of the most difficult ways to disappear and comes with a litany of legal ramifications and problems for you when you get caught. Notice I said when, it will happen.

It does not matter if you are even in another country when you "die". Take for instance the story of Modolvan citizen Igor Vorotinov (Google it to find the story). He got a policy for $2 million dollars when he was in Minnesota in 2010. A year later he went to Moldova that's a small place between Russia and Ukraine, and faked his death with the body of someone else and had someone from the US embassy and his wife verify the body as his. They cremated the body, got a death certificate, and his wife came home to cash in the policy.

In 2013, the FBI received a tip that the guy was still alive, and upon his son and his son's fiancée traveling to and from Modolva, they confiscated his computer to find pictures of the dead guy alive and well. They also found wire transfers of the proceeds from the insurance settlement sent to a Swiss bank account and confirmed money had been sent to the dead guy. Point being that, if this guy with years of planning this, leaving the country for a third world place to pretend die, and one tip starting up the search for him led to him being found and arrested, what do you think your chances are?

This leads me to one of the most important facts of disappearing that you must abide by. Do it alone!

If you are planning on taking a child, even one not in school, rethink your plan. Eventually you will be found. For a child to be raised properly they must have a stable home to grow up with a stable family. If you disappear, chances are you will be somewhat nomadic especially in the beginning, and a child has a hard time with that. If there is another parent involved with the child and you kidnap them, they will never stop looking for you. You can also be arrested if you are taking them illegally. If your kids are older, they will try to contact their family and friends and you will be caught no matter how well you train them.

You cannot be with your children 24/7 and this is what it would take to run with them. If you are running from a bad situation, there are plenty of places to run for safety without disappearing. Look into your options first. Look at law enforcement if you are in an abusive relationship or have a stalker, or even if you are a gang member or ex-cult member looking to get out of the life. Women's shelters, the Salvation Army, churches, and other places can help those in need. Witness protection programs apply to those in certain situations. Make sure you have covered all your bases before deciding that running and creating a new identity is the thing for you and your kids.

Another thing that you must consider is your animals. Some of you may have a dog or cat and the thought of sending them to a shelter or adopting them out makes you cringe and breaks your heart. Traveling with animals are much more difficult because you must care for them and meet their needs while you are bouncing around and not stable. The best option is to get rid of them because this is one more burden of escaping. If you feel you can't then you must have more time to prepare to leave. If you must get out immediately, and don't have time to set up your new life, then this is the only option. I love my cats as if they were one of my kids, it would be difficult for me to part with them. I understand.

Privacy is one of your only friends in this adventure so don't tell anyone ever about your plans to leave, where you are going, and how you are going to do it. If you must suggest to anyone that you are going somewhere like when you are getting ready to leave, tell them somewhere completely opposite of where you are headed. You will learn about planting false leads further in the book.

There are two ways to start over with your identity, legally or illegally. Obviously, legally would be the option of choice for everyone if that is possible. Illegal ways are antiquated and with the communication network between the government and private entities, the ability to go at it illegally is much harder than it used to be. Legally, you can change your name through the court system, this is an option. Understand though that your basic American identifier, your Social Security number will stay the same. If anyone catches wind of you changing your name, they can easily slip into the courtroom during your name changing hearing and have your new name to find you.

If you are thinking about going at it illegally, be very careful and do everything on your own and for yourself. Fake names and identification abound on the internet, they can be easily bought. These are not like the people you see on the series Breaking Bad though that had to pay $125,000 to get the new paperwork and IDs to escape Albuquerque. Most of these on the Internet are scams in one fashion or another and you will either get caught because they sell the same identity multiple times, or send you documents that look like a teenager typed them up.

Many also "sell" you a fake identity and once you've paid, you will never get what you paid for. Also think about going to a bank, dealing with law enforcement, or even going to the DMV or Social Security office to get new paperwork based on false or fictitious documents. These people are trained to look for suspicious people that are nervous, sweaty, avoiding eye contact, mumbling through misinformation, and showing other signs of deceit and lies. Keep in mind that the Social Security offices has armed guards situated at the front door to heighten your nervousness.

The fake IDs or paperwork you get could also be that of people that have their own litany of problems like criminal records, bad debt, or tax problems. You could get only half information, where some is accurate and some is not that will bring up giant red flags to any place you go to get IDs, licenses, Social Security cards, or other paperwork.

Think of your story too if you decide to try and become a baby that died around the time you were born and trying to believably explain how you were out of the country for years as a missionary, and at 50-years-old decided to come back to America to claim your birthright. How believable would you have to be for that? Take some acting classes for sure.

So, after all that if you are ready to proceed... let's move on

I'm sure you have questions

When I decided to start researching the possibilities of disappearing, my goal was to see if it was really possible. It is. With that I decided to think about all the questions that would come up about disappearing in my mind so that all bases were covered and no one could find me. The main questions were how do I prepare to leave without anyone knowing, where would I go if this were my decision, and how do I create a new life under the radar once I get there. With these three main questions came a lot more that needed answered, so I jotted down a list on a piece of paper then proceeded from there.

You should start too by jotting down all the questions you have to create a starting point. Maybe you have an idea of where you want to go already, you could have a way of making money, or you could have an idea of "who" you want to become when you start over. What you likely don't have yet is the answers to how you are going to accomplish all this and that's why you are reading this.

At this point I want to answer one question that everyone has, which is if it is possible to create a new life and live a "normal" life in society once you leave and reestablish yourself. The answer is yes. Creating a new identity does not mean that you have to run off with the carnival or go live in the woods the rest of your life. You can become a normal functioning, tax paying citizen in your new life, and although you are hidden from your past life you can be a normal person. If you want a life of seclusion, that is your option too. You will live a life that you must lie sometimes, and you will be deceiving everyone you run into.

If you are telling lies that will harm no one, or you are not taking a false oath, where is the real harm? As long as you are not doing something illegal, filing false information on your tax returns, or not signing contracts with illegal information you are good. This can all be done under the guise of your new identity, and you can ask God for forgiveness if you need for the rest. The key is to conceal your identity and that is what you need to do.

Two categories exist in those that need to get out, and preparation is the key. Those are people that need to get out right now and leave, while there are those of you that can patiently wait until you have all your preparations done and plan out your journey to go. If you have to get out now and quickly, your journey will be different than those that have time to plan and prepare.

There are those of you also that need to get out short-term because you are in fear of someone and need to hide. There are those of you that need to get out for a while so you can get yourselves back on track to pay off debt. Maybe you need to take a break from your current self to set up a new business or put money away to get back on your feet. Then there are those that are completely done with this life of yours and you want to permanently become your new self.

Let me say this... if you are escaping because you made poor choices that got you to this point, you must change your attitude, behaviors, and the actions that got you here or you will create your new life and end up in the same place you are today. If it is because of bad money choices, learn how to make better choices. Dave Ramsey is an expert on money management and budgeting, pick up his book.

If you have made poor choices in picking a partner that created a bad situation, learn how to check them out better before you get with them so you are not dating a psychopath. As I said earlier you can search the Internet for people and spend $19.95 at many websites to look at information anonymously to see people's baggage. If you are a criminal, stop doing illegal things. Point being, that whatever you did to get here, don't do it again. There is an old saying that if you continue to do the same things expecting different results this is the definition of insanity. Don't be insane.

How much time it takes you to prepare to leave really depends on your situation. Obviously, if you are someone that owns a home and has strong roots in the community, it will take more time than someone that has no roots and is a loner. Typically, someone that doesn't have time needs to just get out so they will have to sort out these long-term things once they have gone. If you have the time to set up your new life then take it, planning and preparation is the key o success. Typically, three to six months to plan your Day of Vanishing (DOV) is best. Some may take longer; some may take less.

Other questions you must ask yourself before you leave is what to do with your home, work, money, and your online life. I say online life because one of the most important things you must do is get offline. If you own a home you must get your name off it, so sell it. This obviously is for someone that has time to prepare.

You also need to figure out how much cash you should leave with, and this is dependent on where you are going and how you plan to leave. It also depends on how quickly you think you can start making money once you get to your new life. If you can get money coming in immediately compared to taking time to get something set up, this will determine how much cash you will need when you leave.

You have spent some time on this earth, so many of you have possessions that you have accumulated during that time. One of the questions that came to my mind is what do I do with them? The only answer is to get rid of them. If you take anything into your new life from your past life, your chances of being found are greater no matter what they are. If they are sentimental things, too bad. Anything that can out you in your new life is forbidden. This may sound harsh, but survival is key in your journey.

Where you want to go is completely up to you, you may think to yourself what the best places to hide in the world are. Small towns are the worst because everyone knows everyone and is into everyone's business. Big cities are great if that your thing because people come and go all the time and nobody knows nobody. If solitude is your goal, then remote living may be the thing for you. This means no neighbors and no interaction with people.

Tourist places are great too because strangers come in and out all the time. As I said in the first chapter, moving at least 250 miles away from your current community and at least one state away is minimum requirements so that you do not run into anyone that may know the old you. If someone sees you (and they will all know you disappeared) from your past, you will be outed.

You will have to leave to somewhere that nobody knows your name, your face, and your identity. The southern USA is a great idea too because you will have much less to deal with the cold weather and that means less resources to live. If you love the cold and want to head to Alaska, more power to you. Moving to a new country takes things to a whole other level, you have much research to do and it is harder to plan and execute your escape. Going to another country is also easy to track because you have to go through customs to get there.

You also do not want to go to a place that you have ever said you would go to people in your past life. Aunt Sally, when she's asked if she has any idea where you may have gone could spill the beans and say that you have always talked about going to Tampa. Guess what? Someone will look for you there.

Your basic necessities in life will not change when you leave, which is food, water, and shelter. You will have to plan on getting these once you leave, and in today's society that costs money. Unless you are planning to live off the land and become Daniel Boone, you will have to find a way to stabilize your life and support for these things. One note about those thinking about running off to the woods and live off the land. If you are not an expert in outdoor survival, lose that thought. You will get to a point that you will have to interact with society and you will not survive in the wilderness. Unless you have the skills to build your own shelter, purify water, and hunt and forage for your own food, going off into the wilderness long-term is a stupid idea.

Planning your escape too means how do you leave and go to the place of your dreams without getting caught or seen on cameras. You cannot leave a trace of how you went, so planning your escape route and method is instrumental. There are things that you must take when you leave too, and the amount of stuff and what to take is important to figure out based on your time, your resources, and your method. If you have the time to plan and setup your DOV, by all means do this. The more time you take and the preparation you do, the easier moving into your new life will be.

When you leave on your DOV, where you go to is also important, along with establishing your income. You can survive while on the cash that you leave with, but eventually it will dry up and paying for motels, along with buying food at restaurants becomes pricey. You also want to stay under the radar and not be seen in public much in the beginning, so having not to go into public is a good idea. You need time to change your appearance once you leave so having a good base with your basic necessities is instrumental. You also want to leave with cash or prepaid credit cards when you go because banking is off the radar for a while when you leave. Both cash and prepaid cards is a way to spend money without giving up your true identity to others.

Now comes the fun part, start planning your new life...

Let's get your journey started. First rule, is that your plan is your secret and you must not talk to anyone about it. Trust no one with your secret. My suggestion is to get out a pen and paper to start making your plan, as I said earlier, anything you do on your home computer is something someone can find at a later date. No matter what program you use or how you try to hide what you are doing on your home computer someone can find it. Also, a good idea is to go spend $20 and get yourself a good shredder or have a burn barrel in the back yard to make all your paper disappear once you are done with your planning. If you are using a pad of paper you want to destroy the whole thing when you are done because writing causes indents on the next pages that someone can find.

You also do not want to make all your changes at the same time in the suggestions that are coming next. If you stop talking to family, disappear from online social media, get rid of your living arrangements, close your accounts, and sell your car all at the same time, someone in your life will suspect you are up to something. Be methodical in your planning and execution to keep from arousing any suspicion. You should get offline and start eliminating all your information that is on there. Start with your social media accounts as these are places that people can find out a lot of information about you.

Facebook has become a home to all your information because they have areas on your profile to tell everyone else about you. From your birthdate to your employment, to the books you like to read and the movies you like to watch. They also have a documented history of your life since joining through the pictures you post online and the posts that you make. If you are questioned by anyone about why you left social media, simply tell them you are tired of the drama and bullshit that is on your news feed and needed a break. They will not know if you inactivated or deleted your account, of course you want to delete it.

This goes for all other social media accounts too. Keep in mind too that if you delete a social media account, they normally will have a grace period before it is actually gone. This could be 30 or 60 days. You want to make sure that you are through this grace period before you take off because if you leave and this period is not up, someone can fake being you and reopen them to gather information on you.

Close all your social media accounts, and make sure that they are gone. Any other accounts you have through websites need to be shut down too. Most websites that you belong to either have a way on the website to cancel your account, phone number to call to cancel your account, or an address to physically mail a request to cancel your account. You also want to search yourself online to see the places that have your information. Most social media sites will let you "delete" your profiles and will still hold onto all the information there for about 10 years before it is expunged off their servers.

Start with a simple Google search of your name and current location, then start eliminating as much as you can about yourself through those sources. It is your information, so getting in touch with those websites and asking them to remove your information usually works. Go a step further then and pay one of those people search websites to dig up all the information on you they can find. This is a good thing because it will lead you to places that you would not think to look to eliminate your information. Unless it is public records, you can have it eliminated.

On top of eliminating your social media presence is another option if you want to take it a step further. You can actually remove yourself from websites that compile your data that people search for information on you. It is a time consuming and tedious process, but worth it if you want to get your information off the Internet. Each one has an opt-out process that you can use to take your information down. This is a good idea if you are temporarily vanishing and want to return to your old life someday. Websites are also out there that will eliminate your information on these people search websites for a fee. This can take away the headache of you doing all the leg work yourself if you don't mind a fee.

Another thing you can do with the information you cannot get rid of is to change the details on those accounts that will stay no matter what you do. This can be by modifying your name, address, phone number, or email address on those accounts so nobody can link them back to you if someone calls the websites looking for information on you.

You can get in contact with those companies and websites and update your information with them by providing them with incorrect information to put into their databases. Some with require you to enter a code sent via an email or with a text to a new phone number. You can easily get around these by setting up a fake email account or by purchasing a burner phone. Both of these options will be discussed later in the book.

One note now that you are removing yourself from the Internet is to stop allowing people to take pictures of you. You do not want any recent photos of you as you are nearing your DOV because this will make it easier for you to be caught. Stay away from the camera so that you will not be seen in a recent photo. Many friends and family will post your pictures online even without your knowledge if you are at a social gathering or somewhere else that involves others. This has become prevalent in today's society because everything must go online.

Another thing that you must do starting now is to distance yourself from your co-workers, associates, friends, and family. Again, if you suddenly stop talking and hanging out with everyone abruptly, this will raise a red flag. This will also be your first true test of how committed you are to getting into your new life. The reason this is, is because you are going to have to start making excuses and telling lies to the people that you care about to start distancing yourself. Stop going out to the bar to have a beer with your co-workers, stop going to dinner with your friends, stop going to cookouts with your family, be too busy to go out on a date with your girlfriend. Stop going to church, and stop going to groups that you belong to.

Do this gradually over time instead of all at once, I cannot reiterate this enough. If you go to church for instance, miss a Sunday then go back, then miss a couple Sundays and go back. At first people will question you about your absences and you will have to make up excuses and lies, but over a period of time they will stop asking you.

If you have a significant other, this can become tricky, especially if they think things are going great. You need to decide whether it is best to start distancing yourself from them or if it a better option to pretend like everything is normal up to your DOV. You will have to decide what the best way to handle your specific situation, the most important thing is to ensure that they have no idea what you are planning to do. If distancing yourself would raise suspicion, a ruse might be the best option.

Eliminating your online life and stopping the social aspect of your life will start giving you two things. It will start putting distance between you and those around you, and it will give you much more time to plan and do the activities you need to do to vanish. Another thing that can give you more time is to stop doing your leisure activities and hobbies. If you come home from work and surf the Internet for hours while watching your favorite flick on television, stop doing these. Everything in your life now is about being ready for your DOV, and the more time you have in your day will help you be prepared.

So, let's talk about preparations…

How do I prepare to leave?

Preparing to leave is about disconnecting from your old life, and setting up your new life. As discussed earlier, you want to be methodical in your planning and working to get to your DOV. I suggest you take a look at a few different things before setting your DOV.

To conduct your research online and doing it anonymously while you are planning there are a couple steps you can take that will help conceal your identity. You will want to get a new computer so it is not tied to you, your home, or your identity. Of course, do not use your personal credit card to buy it so you can remain undetected. You can get a cheap computer from places like Walmart or other stores that will run you $100 to $150. One recommendation is to go to a store you normally wouldn't go to for the purchase, even go a few cities over so that if anyone ever thinks to search the videos of your normal store you won't be there.

You could also use places like Craigslist that you can buy someone's old computer cheap and you meet them in a public place and do the exchange with no personal information given back and forth. Be careful of Craigslist though because there have been stories of people getting robbed by the seller. You could also be purchasing a stolen computer from them. Make sure you are in a public place with other people around to make the exchange. For added security park your car out of sight so they cannot get any information on you.

Once you have your computer, you want to stay incognito online and simply opening a private browser will not keep people from seeing you. Each computer that accesses the Internet has an IP address that identifies that computer and you want to keep that hidden. If an IP is linked to you, it can be easy to find you. Any law enforcement or hacker can do that quickly. Do not use any Wi-Fi that requires a login to access, there are many free Wi-Fi spots around town that you can easily jump on without giving your information to them.

Also use a proxy server like TOR when you are accessing the web. You want to do this because a proxy server will keep your IP address hidden while you are online from anyone. You will want to combine this with a Virtual Private Network (VPN) to stay completely incognito. This is an app that you install to completely obliterate your IP address when used in conjunction with TOR from anyone anywhere finding out who you are, including the government.

If you do not hide your IP address while surfing the web, someone somewhere can track you and with the IP and find out who you are and your location. You suggest that no one knows who bought the computer, so how would they find you? Better to take extra precautions than to have the possibility of being found. Tor or other type services like this combined with a VPN will keep you from being tracked because it makes the Internet think you are in multiple different locations and uses multiple IP addresses that are not yours rather than the one you are actually at and the one you are using. You can also communicate anonymously, and send files and information anonymously. You can learn easily how to use TOR and a VPN through various places, and once installed you can be invisible.

The big question in planning your DOV is where exactly you are going. As discussed earlier, if you do not already have a destination in mind, remote places, big cities, and tourist destinations are a good starting point. Determine what kind of climate you want to be in, and what type of environment suits you best.

When thinking about where I would want to go if leaving the Midwest, to start with it cannot be anywhere like a desert because of the lack of grass would bother me. Then, a warmer climate would be ideal and a big city would not be my favorite. Think about your likes and dislikes and narrow down the climate, weather, type of living that would fit you best, and that will start narrowing down where you should end up. Also keep in mind your resources because if you live in North Carolina for instance and your ideal place to go is California you would need a few hundred dollars in gasoline or a bus ticket alone to get there.

Next you want to figure out the type of living arrangements you would want. When you are moving initially to your new area, you want to be modest and frugal until you get yourself setup and established. Hotels are more expensive than other places, and most of them require ID to stay in them. You can locate very inexpensive local motels that you can pay cash for and some do not require an ID, although those places are normally nasty holes in the wall and the neighbors are at the very bottom of the social scale typically.

A good idea is to set yourself up with a motorhome or travel trailer if you have the means, some people even go as far as buying a used box truck and go "stealth mode" for their living. You can also look for rooms for rent, or small apartments that are for rent by owners that wouldn't require much in the form of identification. Some even escape and use a tent or sleep in cars to get away.

Keep in mind that whatever you chose to become your "home" when you leave, you must remain inconspicuous to those around you, even law enforcement. Research where you would stay if you are not thinking about a motel, small apartment or house, or a room to rent. If you decide for instance to sleep in your car, always keep in mind that police officers driving around will stop and check on you if you are not at a place like a truck stop that something like that would be common. Travel trailers and box trucks are a little less susceptible to that, although if it looks out of place, they will check it out. If you decide to tent camp, keep in mind the wildlife too, and that you are not someplace that people will intrude into your privacy.

You also want to think about how you are going to get from where you are to where you are going. This too depends on how far away you are going. You will avoid planes and trains as the government keeps good records of who is flying and riding on trains. If you are going on a bus, you will pay with a prepaid credit card that does not tie back to you. Do not take cabs when you leave because they keep records of pickup and drop off addresses, and the drivers will be able to possibly describe you as one of their riders. The same is true about companies like Uber and Lyft.

Public transportation is a good way to get away too because you do not have to identify yourself to use them. Remember though that they typically have cameras on those busses or subways so you will have to change your appearance when you take off on your DOV. Remember too that the mode of your escape determines what you can carry with you when you leave too, so if you want to take more than can fit into a backpack, you will need to have some type of transportation to take it with you.

Some people even leave on foot, or on a bicycle that is not necessarily a bad idea because these ways cost nothing to use and you need no identification or license to do either. Do not hitchhike though, because you never know what crazy you may run into if you get in someone's vehicle, and when going down the road at 70 miles per hour you have no way of escaping should you need to.

A note about buying vehicles... you will learn in the next chapters how to buy a vehicle without having it tied directly to you. You can also buy a cheap vehicle from an individual and a lot of times they will allow you to drive off with their license plate and registration until you can get your own. Take advantage of this because this will allow you to get away fast and far and not be found.

You must make sure that all the lights work, the windshield is not broken, it is not smoking, it is not loud (leaking muffler), and that the turn signals are working. You also must make sure the car has no tracking system, or disable the tracking system before your DOV so the vehicle cannot be tracked when you leave. Anything that would draw the attention of a police officer is a no-no. Also do not buy a stolen vehicle, your seller must have the title and give it to you. Verify the title to the numbers on the vehicle and the registration, including checking the plate to the registration.

Understand too that this is a car that you plan on only using, because when you get away you will abandon it. Don't take it to your final destination since it can be tied back to tracking you down. I suggest doing this if you plan on going to a far destination. Take it only so far then find another means to get to your final destination. If you have the funds and ability, you can also use this as a scheme to throw off would be trackers. You could buy a vehicle, drive the opposite direction of where you are going, hop a bus to the location you want to go, and people will be looking for you where the car was left. You could also do this with your personal vehicle if you don't mind losing it's worth.

Never try to lease a car or borrow one from a friend or family member, these can easily be tracked if you are spotted. We will also discuss later in the book ways to purchase a vehicle without you having your named directly tied to it.

Depending on where you are going will determine how you are going to make money when you vanish. Also, the amount of time it will take you to get income will help determine your living arrangements. When you leave and are starting out in your new location, the location you are in will help determine the type of work you will be doing. To stay under the radar, you will want to start in cash type jobs, or menial positions that do not require identification and can pay you cash.

Some types of jobs that you can get are temp jobs, construction, farms, cash paying jobs, gigs, freelancing, photography, writing, handyman, food, or carnival jobs. Craigslist is a good place to find these types of jobs. Starting your own business is a great idea too so you can be in control of the income you bring in.

Other jobs that you can do could be handyman work, painting houses or commercial, office or home cleaning, landscaping, storage unit auctions, or driving jobs. You could move travel trailers from one part of the country to another, or use shipping websites to get shipping gigs that pay cash primarily.

If you need to learn a new skill to be able to make money, a great place to go is www.udemy.com. This website is all about training and you can learn about anything. The great part about it too is that you can pay for classes that teach you all you need to know in one class for only $10 to $15. It's a cheap way to get the knowledge you need to start a new career. There are many classes that teach you how to make money online, such as becoming a life coach, building websites, or doing online marketing.

My suggestion is to take more money with you than you think you will need, because something could happen along the way and cause you to spend more money than you thought you would need. If you are leaving on your DOV and have no income coming in when you leave, then you are going to need to be prepared. What if you currently have no money? Then take the time to get yourself prepared. Many people get caught or fail at vanishing because their resources dry up before they have an income.

There are a few ways that you can save and make money to put away for your DOV. First, as mentioned above, stopping doing anything social will help you save money on top of distancing yourself from others because you are not spending the money that you would if you kept going out.

If you are in a relationship or living with a significant other, you can tell them you are going out. Don't actually go out, rather stash the money in a safe hidden place and work on your preparations. Be careful though to not get caught up in a lie because if they find out you have not been hanging out with your buddy Joe when you said you were, they will think you are up to something.

Also, get rid of all your bills if you can except the ones that provide you food, water, and shelter. Everything you are doing in your life now is preparing you for your DOV. As I stated earlier, you are taking none of your possessions with you so sell off everything that you can. Craigslist is a good place to sell things that will put cash in your pocket. Also make sure your credit cards have no debt and the cards are destroyed and the accounts are closed.

If you have sentimental things or family things that you do not want to sell or give away, make sure you plan and prepare to have them gone by your DOV without anyone knowing that you are leaving. You can even put them in a Rubbermaid tub and drop them off just before you are leaving at a friend or family member's house. Leave it on the back porch in the middle of the night if you must. Just remember though that this will throw up red flags that you are gone and the more time you put in between leaving and people finding out, the easier it is to get away. You could even get a small storage unit and mail the key and code to them in the worst-case scenario.

tart taking money out of your bank account(s) slowly and over time until they are all emptied. Just like when you are owly and methodically distancing yourself from people, take small amounts of money out over time as to not raise any ed flags. Take money out of your 401(k) if you need to because that is usually a place where people have large sums. his will come with early withdrawal penalties and tax repercussions, and do this only if you are leaving your old life ermanently.

o on a frugal diet for now and stay away from restaurants that are expensive. The average man needs about 2400 alories a day to live and an average female needs about 2000. Get rid of your cable, Internet, or any other extras that ost you money.

o find a part-time job if you are working full-time already and stash everything away you make from that. You can find rork from home jobs that you can do on your computer now that you have freed up your time to prepare for your DOV.

you have the ability, find a way to lower your living expenses even more. If you can get out of your home or apartment nd rent a room from someone this can lower your monthly expenses tremendously. This also has another thing that rill positively impact you, which is getting all utilities out of your name. It will be easy also for you to leave a situation ke that because most of the time you rent week to week or month to month and the utilities are in their name. Do not ver room with family, friends, or acquaintances because this can put your plans in jeopardy. The goal is to distance ourself from the people you interact with regularly and keep your secret a secret. Living with one of these people will ake that almost impossible to do.

1ake sure by time of your DOV that all your utilities are paid off and out of your name. This is also true of your rental greement or mortgage if you have one. Of course, these people will come looking for you if you leave without doing so, nd the more that come looking the greater chance you have of being found.

he last thing you want to do before leaving on your DOV is to sell your vehicle. This can be another place that you can et significant cash depending on what the year, make, and model of the vehicle is. Sell it lower than market values if ou must to get rid of it quickly. Leaving in your own vehicle to disappear is one of the stupidest things you can do ecause you can be tracked easily.

ne of the last things you want to do is to shut off your cell phone service and telephone. If you take your current cell hone with you, it can and will be traced even if you shut it off. With today's technology, companies can locate you herever you are with them, and it is easy for them to do. Don't do it until the last possible moment though because his will raise red flags to those that normally call, text, or communicate with you through the one you have.

bviously, if you are in a relationship and living with a significant other, some of these suggestions will not work for you. ake what you can from the suggestions and do what you must to put money away. You will have to start hiding things om your significant other now to make things happen secretly.

you are running from debt, running from a law suit, or something else that will hinder you doing these things then you an't. These are all suggestions that can help your escape easier without people looking for you. If for instance, you just eed some cash to get away from debt and you are going into hiding for that reason, you can walk away from your life ithout shutting it down like I have described above.

his brings me to an important topic too. You are doing everything secretly, and don't want anyone to know what you re doing. If you plan on leaving on a bicycle with a backpack and tent, you can easily hide these things almost in plain ght from others and they will not suspect anything. On the other hand, if you plan on getting a car, getting an RV or uying a box truck to leave in on your DOV you are going to need a secret place to put that stuff and accumulate what ou need.

1

Look online for garages for rent or finding someone that will rent you a piece of property for cash is your best option. You must keep everything you are accumulating for your new life hidden from your present life period. Do not disclose your true identity to those you rent from, and try not to rent in a place that is close to where you live. Again, if someone spots you, your secret is out.

Let's talk about what you should take with you...

What do I take with me?

The short easy answer to this question is cash, because you are going to need enough to survive until you have some money coming in again. The start of your journey after your DOV is going to be a frugal one unless you are strapped with all the money you need. This is the biggest reason for planning and preparation in leaving your current life. The biggest thing that you need to make sure of when you leave is you can provide those three basic necessities that I suggested earlier. These again are food, water, and shelter.

By now you should have your decision on where you are going to go, and how you are going to get there based on your choices and means to make it happen. The following will be a comprehensive list and the list will start with those wanting to take off on foot or a bicycle and we will work up to those that are wanting to leave in a vehicle to and RV or box truck. Some basic things will be the same throughout. One of your questions might be how much it is going to cost you, and the best suggestion I can give is to come up with a budget for your DOV and go from there.

If you are going to leave on a bicycle, the ability to carry things you need are going to be limited, so you are going to need a lot of cash to get them on the go. You can for the short-term pack a tent and some basic hygiene gear, along with a water filtration device and a means to gather some food in the woods.

Remember earlier though I said that if you are going to try to hunt and forage for food, you should have much knowledge and experience to survive outdoors. I have watched Mountain Men and Alaska: The Final Frontier, and this is a lot of work to do. The average person does not have the skills to do it.

At minimum you should prepare a go bag. If you watched these series Dexter that I talked about earlier, you saw the one he had hidden in his wall during the last season. A go bag is essentially a back pack or a duffel bag that you can grab when you hit the door to get out of Dodge. The essentials that you need is a comprehensive list, so you pick and choose from it what matters to you. I will provide examples and the reasons why you need them as follows:

Clothing -
Socks: These are essential because you need to have clean, dry socks to keep your feet healthy
Underwear: Your private parts sweat and can be a haven for bacteria so you need these to stay fresh
Good Boots or Shoes: If you are walking or leaving on a bicycle, you need a good pair to keep from getting blisters and to keep your feet dry.
Pants or shorts: Depending on where you are going you are going to need a couple pair of these
Tee-shirts: A few of these to keep dry and refreshed.
Sweatshirt: Take this to keep warm or a light jacket
Baseball Hat: You will always want to wear a baseball hat when you leave to conceal your identity
Rain Poncho: I would suggest a good one if you are going to be out in the weather
Winter Jacket, Hat, and Gloves: If you are going where the cold weather is, you'll need them

Hygiene Gear –
Bar of Soap: To keep clean and it is compact and lasts a long time compared to liquid
Toothbrush and Toothpaste: Dental hygiene
Towel: Whatever size you can easily carry to dry off (especially your feet)
Wash Cloth: To wash thoroughly
Razor and Shaving Cream: You can take an electric razor (lighter and lasts longer) if you can plug it in
Comb: Lightweight and small
Compact Mirror: Can also be used to start fires
Deodorant: Stick lasts longer than gel
Nail Clippers: Just one for both toes and fingers
Female Menstrual Needs: For your time of the month

Medical Supplies –
Medical Kit: Your best bet here is to take a small one with band aids, gauze, tape, antibiotic ointment, pain medication, and stomach medication
Prescription drugs: If you are on them, you need a few month's supply because it will be a while before you get more

House Supplies –
Fork and Spoon: Metal
Plate and Bowl: Metal
Canteen or Water Bottle: You always want to stay hydrated. If you get a military style canteen, they typically come with a metal pot in the same shape of the canteen you can cook in and eat out of
Water Filtration: You can either get tablets to put in water or a water filter system (The filter is the best bet because tablets will run out, and take couple extra filters if you are going to be off grid for a long time)
Small Cast Iron Skillet: You can cook anything in cast iron
Hunting Knife: For cutting up food and protection
Fishing Twine: If you plan on living outdoors and catching your own food, also take a bag of hooks and sinkers. You can use a stick like they did in the old days.
Ziplock Bags: I would take some of these to keep your small items dry both small and large bags
Flashlight: To see in the dark
Waterproof Matches: To start fires (also take a lighter, magnifying glass, and fire-starting flint so you have multiple ways to start a fire)
Knife Sharpener: To keep your knife sharp
Rope: To hang up wet clothes to dry and to help with shelter
Portable USB Solar Charger: These come in handy for small devices
Sewing Kit: To repair your clothes

Camping –
Tent: To get out of the weather
Sleeping Bag: Best bet for compact warmth
Compass: For direction
Maps of the United States: For details of where to go
Small Folding Shovel: To dig fire pits and help clear your campsite
Small Axe: To get firewood

Tools –
Portable Car Jumper: Can be used to jump a car and some have outlets to plug into
Bicycle Repair Kit: If you are traveling by bicycle
Socket Set: If you are traveling by vehicle
Screw Drivers: Flat and Phillips
Pliers: Basic pair (Also could get a pair of pliers with tools in the handle)
Stanley Knife: Useful tool
Zip Ties: These come in useful
Lockpick Kit: You made need to get into some place you don't have keys for

Car Supplies –
Remember that when you take a car you do not want to stuff it full like you are a hoarder because this will raise suspicion with law enforcement. Only put things in the trunk primarily.

RV or Box Truck Supplies –
When you prepare a RV or box truck you can start with a hammock, 5-gallon bucket to relieve yourself, and some type of water container up to fully converting these to be livable dwellings. You can search YouTube for videos about how to fully convert a box truck into stealth mode.

Another thing about leaving in a box truck is you can buy a magnetic sticker for the doors or the side of the box with a company name and logo that will make your truck look like a business vehicle. You could also paint this on if you have the ability.

Food –

There are so many directions you can go with food when you leave. If you are walking or on a bicycle you can take high protein energy bars, or military meals ready to eat. If you are in a car you can carry more, and in an RV or box truck you can stockpile non-perishables to get you through a few months.

So now that you have your destination, mode of travel, and items to bring, you should be able to come up with your budget. If you are planning on leaving on a bicycle and living in a tent, you could easily do this for a couple thousand dollars and last a few months. If you plan on living in a fully converted box truck you can spend up to $15,000 for the truck, conversion, gas, and food. If you can take the time to gather these things before your DOV, you can have less money that you need to stockpile.

For instance, if you can take a year to prepare and convert a box truck, you can be fully ready and need only money for gas and food. If you are planning on getting a vehicle and finding a place to rent once you get to your destination you will need up to $10,000 cash with you to last a few months. In any case, you will need to adjust your needs, find a way to make more money, give yourself more time to prepare, or adjust your plans to make it all work.

By this point you should know where you want to go, how you are going to get there, what type of transportation will take you there, and your living arrangements when you arrive. You will also have figured out how much you need to save to successfully vanish, and started considering how you are going to accumulate the money or things you need to vanish.

One of the most important things you will want to do is to get your passport if you do not have one. You will see later on in the book why this is important. Do this before your DOV so that you have it when you leave. You can go to post offices, clerks of court, public libraries and other state, county, township, and municipal government offices to obtain it. Go to the Department of State website to find the location closest to you to get it.

With budget in mind, personal things resolved, and time it will take you to be prepared, you should now have an idea of when you can vanish. At this point you should set your official DOV and implement your plan to be ready for that day.

Let's talk about the new you…

Creating My New Identity

Your new identity is important to create because this is going to be who you become. When you vanish, you need to implement the changes you decide immediately to conceal yourself. This is not some acting gig that you will pretend to be your new self, rather it is who you actually are. You must get rid of your old self in appearance, mannerisms, habits, likes, hobbies, and even the foods you like.

Remember, you are working towards becoming unidentifiable as the old you, so you must become something different. You could take it a step further and even change the way you walk and talk, like if you typically walk around with a frown on your face you could change that to a smile.

When you leave on your DOV, you don't want any suspicion that you are trying to hide something to the new people you come in contact with, so it is important to "become" the person you are going to be. This is an effort to never get caught by being the person you were. You may have to act in the beginning and fake it until you make it before this becomes second nature. You are starting with a clean slate so you can be whoever you want.

The first thing I want to talk about is when it comes to you is your appearance. This is obviously the most outright thing you can change to not be detected. You want to make sure on your DOV that you leave everything behind, including your clothes. If, for instance, you liked to dress in polo shirts and dockers, you want to leave in tee shirts and jeans.

Go to the store and get some new clothes while you are preparing for the new you. You can even go to Goodwill or the Salvation Army stores to find clothes cheap. Do not get anything too eccentric or that would make you stand out because you want to blend in with your new environment. If you are going to a rural area, you don't want to dress in a suit and tie because you will stand out like a sore thumb.

The next obvious thing is your face and your hair, that can be easy to change. Create a new hairdo for yourself, whether it be cutting your long hair or growing out your short hair. Change the color of your hair by dying it and make sure it is a natural color that doesn't stand out. If you are a guy, grow a beard if you have none or cut your beard off if you do. You can also gain some weight or lose some weight when you vanish and this will help reduce the ability to detect you.

Always wear a baseball hat because this will help conceal your face from cameras. Sunglasses are a good coverup too if the weather is appropriate and would look normal. One thing to note though that sunglasses are normally useless against facial recognition cameras because these facial recognition systems use about 80 points on the face to determine who someone is. They can use as little as five points to make that determination.

One thing that can help in public places is to be looking down as you are moving along because cameras are normally above you looking down on you. Another thing you can do at night is to wear one of those clip-on lights for the bill of your baseball cap that will totally hide your face by glaring light into the camera, although this may not be a conspicuous thing to do. This will cause a glare in any camera like an ATM, so there will be no way to identify you. Low light is better to reduce the ability of cameras, as is wearing a hood of a sweatshirt if it is appropriate. So night time is the best to go out when you need to in the beginning.

A good idea too is to change your mannerisms in your new persona. This can be the way that you walk, if you use your hands a lot to talk, or things that you may say regularly out of habit. You might be a fast eater and you want to slow down. Even change your favorite foods and try different ones, and go to different restaurants than you normally would. Your current hobbies need to go away, along with other interests. Some people have been located because after they changed their identity, they decided to get a magazine subscription they had in their past life of a hobby they were interested in and were tracked down and found because of that subscription.

ou also want to create a new name for yourself that is a normal sounding common name. When it comes to names in merica, stay away from Mexican names or Middle Eastern names because unfortunately these will raise red flags with any people, especially law enforcement. A good choice is to go with a European name and one that is popular.

his does not mean popular in the sense that a celebrity has it, you want to stay away from known names. This means ames that are popular in culture and if someone did a search for you under your new name, they would find 500 in the ig city you are in. This makes it more difficult for people to look into you with your new identity when you get to your ew location.

good idea before your DOV is to go out into public in your current life and introduce yourself in your new name to see ow easy it is, and how well it rolls off your tongue. Make sure you are not anywhere that someone that knows you will alk up and say your true name, this would be embarrassing and could blow your plans.

Vhen you create a new name, you will also need to practice signing it for when places require a signature. You want to ecome like a doctor, who scribbles out his or her signature and it looks just like that, a scribble. You don't want to have recognizable signature especially because you may have more than one identity in the long-run.

ome of these things suggested in changing yourself may seem trivial and maybe even silly. You are; however, ompletely disappearing from your current life, and want to have no chance in your new life of being found out for who ou are. You do not ever want to be put into a position that you could be found out not matter how slim the chance. kely, if you hold on to some of the things in your past, no one would ever out you for your true identity, but do you now what that one thing is? Doubt it.

ou are also doing this move not only to get away from your old life, you are also doing it to reinvent yourself into who ou always wanted to be. Take advantage of this time and opportunity to do just that and remake yourself in the image ou always wanted to be.

ext, you want to create your story. Along with changing your appearance, mannerisms, habits, likes, hobbies, and ods, you also need to create your new life story. You want to make a new background for yourself that you tell the ew people you will meet. One good way to easily do this is to mix in the background information from someone you now because you will easily recall the details if you are questioned. When you meet new people, you want to have a ood history of your life, and you want it to come out without sounding made up. You always want to tell the same story people in your new life because you are going to start having new acquaintances and friends. You do not want to be aught up between two people with different stories that you told.

few basic things that you want to be able to tell people in your new life are –

Vhere did you come from and what type of work did you do before?
Vhere did you work before you came to your new place?
Vhere is your family and why don't you talk to them anymore?
Vhat kind of food do you like?
Vhat is your favorite beverage to drink?
Vho is your favorite author and musician?
Vhat is your favorite television show and movie?
Vhat are your hobbies?
Vhat is your religion, do you practice?
Vho is your favorite football, baseball, and basketball team?
o you have any kids?
Vhat is the history of your relationships?
Vhy did you move to your new place and chose that place specifically?
Vhat is your educational background and work experience?

2

These are a few answers you will need to think of and there are many more. Create believable, real stories and practice memorizing these things before your DOV so that you have them at the tip of your tongue when asked.

By this point you have made all the decisions about your new life including where you are going, how you are going to get there, the budget you need, and the things you need to take with you. You should have your plan to accumulate the things you need for your DOV and cash to escape, along with a place to hide the things you are accumulating in preparation. You have chosen your new name, and decided on who you are going to be along with the back story and life story of the new you. While you are going through the days of preparation, work on memorizing all the details you must have for your new life.

You should also take the time to gather up your pertinent documents like your social security card, passport, birth certificate, tax returns, bank statements, and other documents you need. You will want these all in one place so you can grab them when you are ready to leave. Anything that has your name, social security number, or photo on it needs to be gathered. When you vanish, destroy the ones that are no longer necessary and stash the necessary ones in a safe place that no one can find them.

You do not want someone to be able to find out who you really are in your new environment so you will need to keep them hidden. If you live with a significant other and do not want to be obvious, you can leave them in a normal place like a file cabinet and consolidate them into one file if you are able. When your DOV arrives, you do not want to be scurrying around unprepared and without all your documentation together.

To escape successfully you will need to plant false leads, which is basically leading anyone that will be looking for you to a place different than you will be going. If you are planning on vanishing to Florida, make them think you went to California. To do this, you want to leave some "crumbs" for them to find.

This is a good opportunity to jump back on your home computer and do searches for your false place and research going there. Look for apartments, jobs, and even places to see when you are there to give the façade that you are headed that way. You could buy an atlas and tear out the page for the fake vanishing place, and even leave some brochures for the area in a drawer. Search online for flight, train, and bus ticket costs. Look up utilities and license branches in the area as if you are looking to relocate there.

If you are going to have higher level people looking for you with the possibility of them hiring private investigators as we discussed earlier, you can leave even more false trails for them to go down. They will have your credit report to look over, and you can plant information on there. Go as far as to actually apply for apartments and utilities in a fake place make it far away. Whatever place you apply at that will pull up your credit report will put their information on your report when the inquiry is made. This can come to your advantage because you can throw off an investigator by sending him or her on a wild goose chase.

One of the first people to notice you are gone is your employer so you have one of two options to buy you some time. Either request some time off at your DOV so they will not think anything about you not being there, or quit your job if is appropriate for your situation.

Your neighbors may also notice you are gone, so you can simply tell them you are going to be leaving out of town for work, or on a vacation for a couple weeks. You can apply this same tactic to any friends or acquaintances that would wonder where you went. Obviously, you have already established disconnecting from them earlier so there should not be many.

Finally, if you have a significant other, tell them you are going on a business trip, to a conference, or on a fishing trip for a couple days with an old friend. Make it plausible that you will not be able to use your phone, or it will be late in the day that you can contact them. This will buy you some time to get away before any suspicion arises.

When your DOV arrives, it is time to put your plan into action and take off. Do not ever look over your shoulder and stress about everyone you see wondering if you are on the run. You are not on the run, because you are now your new identity and you are simply going home to your new home. Most people in society are so worried about what is happening in their own lives they have little time to pay attention to strangers as long as you don't stand out. If you are leaving in a vehicle, take one last trip around it to check that all the lights are working and you will not be noticed by the police.

Now we get to your destination...

Who will be looking for you and how?

When you leave, the clock starts ticking and people will start looking for you. This typically starts with family and friends looking for you, then your work will be called and the people calling will find out you "took a vacation" or you quit before your DOV. If you left false leads, they will start finding them and collecting all the pieces together that will help them determine that you left because you wanted to. This could take a few hours or a couple of days depending on how well you planned your escape and your living situation before you left. If you disconnected completely before your DOV then this will add a lot more time for you to be able to get away.

When you head to your new home, you want to make sure that you are not noticed as being out of place or doing anything wrong as in your driving. Get to your secret place if you have one, collect the things you prepared and head out.

As I said earlier in the book, depending on who you are and what you are running from will determine who will come looking for you and how hard they will look. There are many different methods and means that people can use to find you, and some will try harder than others. One of the first things people will do is to check your cell phone to see if they can use it to locate you. Obviously, you either closed the account or left it behind so that will not work. Then they will search your home computer to see if they can find out any clues as to where you went and they will find a gold mine of the false leads and trails that you left on there. They will also find the atlas and other things you planted to give them a false sense of where you went.

They will also look for transactions on your credit cards and debit cards. This is why you should have paid off and closed those accounts and destroyed the cards. You should have cash or gift cards as your only means to pay for food, gas, and lodging along the way to your destination. If you left in a vehicle, the tank should be full before you leave so the first stop you make will be a few hundred miles away for fuel.

If you are found to have walked away on your own, individuals and companies may hire private investigators to look for you. These private investigators will use any information they can to find you and will use lies and deceit to get the information they need. They get paid based on their results. They will start by searching online with Google and other search engines to locate whatever information they can find on you.

They will also call utilities, phone companies, or any other place that has your information to get leads on how to find you. They will lie to your friends and family, pretend to be you to call places that have information on you to try to get them to tell them where you are, and make up stories to seem plausible as to why they need the information.

They will also target social media accounts you have to gather personal information on you, and this is why you have deleted all these accounts. They will use known email addresses to try to sneak in the back door of these accounts to look at your information. If you deleted these and went through the grace period that you were able to reverse that decision, these will all be gone.

They will use those websites we talked about earlier to get all the information they can on your background and get an idea of where to find you. Obviously, they will get little information because you have told no one of what you are doing, where you are going, and how you plan to get there.

You have also taken the time to completely eliminate as much information online about you as you can. They have underground resources to get information on you that you didn't even know existed. This is why at the beginning of the book I suggested you get offline on your home computer or devices and why you should protect yourself on your new computer and to search online by using a program like TOR and a VPN.

They will search motor vehicle reports, criminal records, and credit reports for your information. If you have any magazine subscriptions, frequent flier clubs, grocery and other store memberships, and any organizations you belonged to they will try to get information from them.

If you purchased how to disappear books from a bookstore, or books on your destination, they can find it if you used your credit card or membership card. Point being, any trace you leave behind can be found by the professional private investigator and they will use any ruse they need to so that anyone from any company will tell them what they need to know. You only have to make one mistake or leave one clue and they can find you.

Another way they will look for you is your vehicle, and you should have sold it already. The police will put out notifications on your vehicle and will be keeping an eye out for it. We will talk in a little bit about how you can purchase a vehicle without it being tied to you so read on.

There are some things that you can do to be outed once you leave too, so you want to avoid doing these things at all costs. Everyone has heard the term "curiosity killed the cat" and you should never be curious. Do not ever look online for any stories about the old you and your disappearance because law enforcement or private investigators will keep an eye out for people searching for themselves. One person went to an Internet cafe after she disappeared and over a few weeks looked up her story online to see if any information was there and after doing that a number of times she was found.

The same is true about the people you left. Do not scour their social media accounts to see what is being said about you because websites like Facebook will have records of who looked at who and this can turn back on you if you take this chance. You left for a reason, and walked away from your old life, so keeping track of what is going on about the old you are not relevant.

The easiest way that someone can be found is to contact the people from their past, even if it to let them know you are okay. If you planted false leads and trails so that people understood that you left because you wanted to, ensured that they had no way to find you, and left unannounced, they will all understand that you are alive and doing well. Leave them be and let them have the understanding that you left them with and move on.

This brings me to one important thing. At the beginning of the book I started by talking about the emotional problems that you will leave people you walk away from. Whether or not you successfully distanced yourself from others, your leaving will impact them. They will wonder why you left, what they did wrong, and what they could have done differently to make you not want to leave. Even if you committed fully to leaving and were determined to start over, part of you might feel some guilt about what you did and how you did it. This is natural and a natural part of the human emotional process.

You probably did not walk away from your old life because everything was wrong or bad for you, although you had enough things wrong that it made this option the only one for you. Work through the grieving process if you have guilt, and constantly remind yourself the reasons you had to make the decision you did. It will get better with time. This is another reason to leave with a few month's supplies or cash, so you can have time to truly wrap your head and heart around the decision you made to completely change your life.

Also, the most difficult part of walking away from your old life is the people you left behind. This was your choice and when you made it, you made it forever. If you try to contact people from your past you will be found, no questions asked. Unless you plan on someday returning to your old life, you should never contact them. If you are returning, only do it when you are ready to be exposed.

How do I stay under the radar?

The only time you will reveal your true identity is for taxes, opening a bank account, and for a police officer if they ask for your license. Other than that, you are going to present the new you and new identity to everyone you meet. We will discuss these three later in the book. This will be a difficult balancing act because you will need to go to places that you will not have to identify yourself to participate. If you smoke or drink, you will have to show your ID to buy cigarettes and alcohol in most places. Some places don't care and don't ask. Learn where you can go and what you can do to keep your identity hidden.

The first thing I want to talk about when it comes to disappearing is to be prepared to disappear again. Once you leave and if ever something goes wrong and someone somewhere finds out that you are not who you say you are, even if they do not learn your true identity, you must be ready to get out as soon as you can.

At minimum, you should have an alternate identity established and ready to go, along with a go bag that is secretly stashed should this time ever come. In this bag minimum you should have a change of clothes, some basic hygiene gear, your information for your alternate identity, and of course a few months supply of cash or prepaid credit cards. This should be your first priority when your start having income coming in for your new life.

Along the way to your destination, you may need to check into a hotel, and you should do so anonymously. As I stated earlier in the book, you should look for hotels and motels that you can check into that are local businesses that you can pay cash at without identifying yourself. Stay away from the big chain hotels because they are much stricter on how you check in. You can also check into local bed and breakfasts, or find one of those websites that have people offer their couches or spare rooms to stay at that require no identification.

If for any reason you must check into a hotel, check into it with a name different than the one that you have chosen for your alternate identity. Use a prepaid card to book the room and pay cash once you get there. Use a ghost address to check in, and tell the person at the counter that you checked in under a pseudonym because you want your true identity to remain confidential.

Most will honor this request and not give out any of your information to anyone, allowing you to keep your identity safe. Many celebrities do this when traveling along with other well-known people. We will talk about ghost addresses later in the book.

If you are in a car, RV, or box truck, you can sleep at rest areas without trouble or at truck stops. If in a car you should probably have some way to cover your windows so no one can look in. I saw a full-size pickup once that had windshield protectors in all the windows to keep prying eyes out and privacy for the occupant. You can also use truck stops to get a shower and they typically offer this with a fill up of gas or for a small fee.

Never reveal your true identity and do not feel comfortable enough to ever settle back into your old habits. You want to make sure that you stay away from places where a lot of people congregate like churches, rallies, groups, or clubs. The more people there, the more will notice you. If your disappearance is on the media, someone could spot you. You should always have only one set of identity documents on you at a time, this is something police will jump on immediately if more than one is found.

One way that people get found too is by predictability. If you do the same things every day, go to the same places, and have the same routine you will start creating a pattern. Switch up your daily activities so you do not create a clear path to you ever. This can be as simple as changing the way you travel to your work. Once you have everything in place in your new life, you will start getting comfortable and that's when people let down their guard. This does not mean you have to live a rigid life, just always be cautious and aware.

ecause you have no record of education and experience, you will have to lie to people about your work history and xperience. If you are trying to get a job and they ask for references, you will need to have a plan. You can walk in with ake letters of references disguised on letterhead that you can easily duplicate on Microsoft Word or Google Docs. Put ame of people on the letters that are people that actually work at the company and put the phone number of one of our burner phones.

ck up a couple prepaid cell phones and disguise your voice to confirm your work experience when people call to check our references. These are commonly referred to as burner phones and they are cheap noncontract phones that you can se for a short time and dispose of. You also want to take the battery and sim card out of them when you are not using hem. We will talk further about burner phones later. Beyond that, you will want to set up a few ghost addresses for ourself if a reference check requires to mail them, or a couple of fake email addresses to email a reference letter to.

ne of the biggest struggles you will run into when you disappear is getting a job. The reason this is, is because when ou work for an employer, you are required to give them your Social Security Number to work for them because the IRS equires that the employer document and record your wages for tax and Social Security purposes.

any require it as a condition to even fill out an application with them so they can run a background and some will run a redit report on you as a condition of employment. You have one option here to keep your information protected, which to tell them that you will give it to them if you are offered a position and not before. If this is not acceptable to them, ove on.

our name, social security number, and address must be submitted to the National Directory of New Hires upon you arting working for them. The only place you can give false information is your address. We will discuss ghost addresses ter in the book. The best option is to have your own business, and try to find a company that you can work for as a ubcontractor rather than an employee. This way, they will pay your company rather than you directly.

When it comes to insurance companies, they do not need to know your Social Security number.

ou have unbanked for now and should stay away from credit completely, staying away from credit is a good way to go n permanently if you can. We will talk about banking anonymously soon, but you want to make sure that you stay nder the radar. Remember, you must live simply for a while, and less is more for your situation. Some temp services nd companies are also supplying debit cards that they put your paycheck on instead of a paper check that will allow ou to access money without having a bank account.

you have not set up your new housing before you left and are planning on finding a place once you get to your estination, there are a few things that you must understand about today's society. Everyone is greedy for information nd details on you so you must choose a place that will look for little. I once applied to rent a house through a property anagement company, and they wanted separate applications for my wife and I including things like birthdate, social ecurity number, residential history, and work history. This is common.

hey also sent me to a website that wanted the date of birth, date of ownership, pictures, and a DNA sample of my two ats to add to their database. This was all under the guise that they wanted to be able to determine who my cats were if hey got lost. Nobody has my DNA, let alone my cat's.

partment complexes are getting just as bad, so stay away from these. You will want to find a house to rent by dividuals that don't ask for much information, or find rooms for rent from individuals. I once found a guy that bought ondos and rented each room out without much information from the tenants. This is communal living, so if you don't ant to do that then find other means to get a place.

o not try to buy a house, and stay away from realtors. These are also people that will ask for all your information to urchase or get into a place. You can look for a seedy motel that will rent out rooms cheap as discussed earlier, just make sure the door locks securely. One way to keep people from asking too many questions is to pay three to six months of rent in advance. This will let the owners know that you are serious about long-term rental and help keep them from asking to many questions.

If you are in an RV or a box truck, stay away from national chain camp grounds because they too are starting to dig deep into people's information. One way to reduce your costs too is to stay in the parking lots of businesses like Walmart or Cracker Barrel that allow travelers to stay for free, rest stops, or at truck stops. Do not stay in one place too long though because they will wonder why you are not leaving. You can use these places though to give you time to find your permanent place to park. Search Craigslist for places that you can go and stay under the radar.

The most obvious thing you should know by having read the earlier parts of this book is to stay off social media sites. These are not a necessary part of living in society, up until 20 years ago we did not have social media. If you start going online again and adding information about yourself even under an assumed identity, people can put pieces together and the process of your privacy going away starts all over again. This will also help you in getting out and living a real life because you won't waste your time on these.

For whatever you do on the Internet, do not every use your old nicknames and identifiers that you did in your old life when creating accounts. Also do not use variations of the same email address when you are creating a new one. For instance, you don't want to set up your first email address identifier as FakeID1@yahoo.con then your second one as FakeID2@yahoo.con and so forth. Be creative and use completely different and unrelated addresses.

Your passwords should all be different and not easily found by someone trying to hack your accounts. The easiest way to do this is something most places on the Internet offers is randomly generated passwords.

You may be wondering how to keep track of all this information that you need to keep track of. Obviously not on some electronic device such as a computer or cell phone, rather you will want to write them down on paper and guard th information with your life. Be cautious with it and do not have it on you at all times, do not want to chance losing it. It must be secure.

Another good idea is to go to the store and pick up a small safe that is fireproof. Your documents and anything important need to stay out of the hands of anyone else so get one that is secure. When you take it home, wherever that is, make sure your put it in a safe hiding place too.

Some people must go online to conduct business, in a few of the recommendations I made earlier in the book about some jobs and even training require you to do so. If you must go online and must set up accounts to navigate your way through, follow the following guidelines. Set up an anonymous email address on each account, and one email address for each one. Getting an email address from a country other than the one you live in will throw off would be information seekers.

When you setup accounts, do it under a pseudonym and without your real information, and use a burner phone if they require a code be sent for authentication. Obviously, anything done on the Internet that requires payment use a prepaid card and do not use your own. If you must put information in such as for a website, make sure to get WHOIS protection and keep as much information from them as you can.

Do not fall back into your old habits or hobbies as people looking for you will be vigilant in looking for you through these. This is why I suggested you create new hobbies and things of interest completely different than your old self. If you have a lot of people looking for you that are businesses or higher level especially, they can hire private investigators that will go through any avenue to find you out.

You also want to stay away from relationships for a while until you are settled into your new life completely and have had a chance to be the new you around other people.

Keep hidden deep under

If you go to a major cell phone company and get a new cell phone, you start leaving a new trail into your life that people can use to find you. If anyone ever finds out who your new identity is, they can easily start calling cell phone companies and dig up information on how to find you. To keep this from happening, you do not want to set up an account with these places, rather you want to get access to a burner phone that is not tied to you.

You can do this by going to a gas station or convenience store and picking up a burner phone. This is a prepaid phone that you can get without having to provide any information to them about your identity. These phones can still be tracked, so you want to make sure the battery is out of them and the sim card too when you are not using them. The best idea is to buy multiple burner phones and use them randomly.

This way, no one phone is ever leaving traces of where you are and it will be difficult to pinpoint your location should someone try. If they do ask for information when you are purchasing your phones, give them fake information and don't give them your ID to verify it. Move on if they must have your ID and find another place to pick one up.

You also want to start using secure email accounts. Using Google Gmail or Yahoo accounts is best because these are SSL accounts. Set up a number of them so that no one email account is used for more than one place. Do not ever make a conspicuous email address or one that would tie you to your old life.

Getting mail at your new address should be avoided, and you should have nothing that comes to that address in the mail. This will help keep anyone from ever knowing your true address by going through your mail. To stay anonymous and underground you will have to set up different ways to get your mail to you.

When you get to your new location and if this is going to be your permanent location, you are going to want to get a Post Office box to receive your mail. It is best to get a PO box that is not within the vicinity of where you are going to be living. To get a PO box the postal service requires two forms of ID with one that has a verifiable address on it. It is illegal to anything otherwise.

When you first move to your new location, you are going to want to get a business set up at a ghost address in the city. You must provide a lease agreement to the Post Office. Take this to the post office with your Passport. Sign up for the PO box and your address stays hidden. You can also do this in a different city than you will be living in. Use your PO Box for everything you can that asks you for an address.

Another option for you that is becoming more commonplace because many people are on the road full-time and a lot of people are living under the radar is using a virtual address. Take advice from people that RV full-time and set yourself up with an address that you can get that is not a PO box or from a UPS store that will give you an actual address without living there. You can use this address as your physical address for licenses and other government required documentation without actually living there. This means you can be anywhere in the country and have an address that is somewhere else.

For any utilities or Internet that you need at your new residence, use the business information to set those up and the PO box as the address for mailing. This will keep your name off the radar for anyone trying to look for you because your name is not on the bill. If someone is searching for you such as a private investigator, they will never know that you are tied to the account if they call.

If you plan on having packages delivered to you from UPS or FedEx, another thing you must do is set up a ghost address. These companies will not deliver packages to the post office and must have an actual physical address to drop them off. To stay under the radar, you are going to want to have an address that is not your own to have these packages delivered to.

Some places that you can look into for a ghost address are small businesses, office buildings with multiple tenants, mom and pop motels, churches, or other type places. The best way to approach these places is to tell them that you travel a lot and you need a place to have packages delivered that you can pick up at periodically. Then offer to pay them "rent" for them to accept the packages. You can get away with as little as $20 a month. This will keep your address hidden from anyone.

For anything that you have coming to you in the mail, you do not want to simply discard it in the trash. People go through other's trash to gather information on them. The two options you have to make sure this does not happen is to either buy a good shredder that cross cuts the documents, or to burn it so that it is destroyed.

One perk that you will also have to forgo to keep your address hidden is food delivery. Today you can have food delivered to your home address easily by using the phone, a web order, and even an app on your phone for a lot of places. Grubhub, Doordash, Uber Eats, and even most pizza or Chinese places will bring food right to your door. If you want to bring restaurant style food home, pick it up yourself.

As I have told you throughout this book, you want to use prepaid cards or cash to make purchases. You can get prepaid cards that can be used anywhere and for almost anything from major retailers and it costs you nothing more than the cash to put on them when you buy them. You can use them the same as any credit or debit card, and the best thing is your name is not on it. One added benefit if you purchase multiple cards is that all your money will not be on one so if you lose it or someone steals it you are not broke.

When you leave, you want to keep your identity a secret, and you also want to do this legally. In the United States, there are only a couple of places and times that you are required to show your driver's license as a form of ID. The main one is when a police officer asks to see your driver's license. To stay under the radar, you do not want to show it other than required.

For instance, if you were to get pulled over in your new life you must provide the police officer with your driver's license. The car you are driving is listed under your company name and address, and your license is from a different state. If a cop were to ask you if you live at that address that is on your license, your can simply elude to the fact that you go back and forth between the place you live and the place on your driver's license.

Use your passport for your identification in every instance that you are not required to show your license. Your passport does not have your address on it and does not have your social security number.

Even when it comes to the government and giving your Social Security number, you have options. With the Privacy Act of 1974, they must tell your four things before you give them the number. First, they must tell you if you are required to give them your social security number, and the statute that requires this. They must also tell you how they will use your Social Security Number. The fourth thing they must disclose is what happens if you do not provide them with it. This will help you determine if you must provide it to them.

If companies "require" you to give them information such as your date of birth or your phone number, give them fake information. Accidentally invert a couple digits of your social security numbers.

Sign up for online billing and payments for any of your bills that you can, most companies will also offer discounts for them not having to send you paper bills. This will help reduce the amount of mail you have being sent to you. Use a separate email address for your bills that you use for nothing else. Anything paper you receive should be shredded or burned so no one can ever see the information.

The easiest way to buy things and not have them tied to you or your address is by creating businesses to place ownership of these things under. You can search online for places you can anonymously start businesses. You will want to put your leases, utilities, vehicles, insurance, and anything else you can into your business. This will keep your name off the information so if someone is looking for you, they will not be able to locate things under your name.

Use your ghost addresses as the addresses for the business too so that your physical location is not found. It is common for businesses to provide vehicles, and to rent housing for employees.

When you must get on the Internet, make sure you do it securely as we discussed earlier. Also make sure you travel a few miles away from your home to access it. Along with using a program like TOR and a VPN, this will add an additional level of protection and security. Also do not go to the same place all the time to use the Internet connection. Also never put your private information like your Social Security Number online.

When it comes to the end of life for your electronics like your cell phones, tablets, or computers you should completely destroy them and not simply throw them away or turn them into a recycling place. These will have your information on them and the only way to ensure no one gets the information is to make sure the device is destroyed.

With the amount of money laundering and scams, banking has become the one place that everyone sticks their nose into and you must give them information that they are required by law to give up to the government if they ask. So, the trickiest part to establishing your new self and stay under the radar is to bank anonymously. The best way to do this is to open a bank account in a business name. If you cash checks, use your passport rather than your drivers license to do so.

This brings me to another point, which is to stay away from using credit. If you disappear and want to stay under the radar you must not apply for or use any credit. Each time you apply for credit including apartment complexes, they run your Social Security number and the credit reporting agencies will document this on your credit report.

As you saw earlier in the book, anyone looking for you including individuals that hire private investigators will use your credit report as a tool to help locate you. Don't do it. You must live on a cash basis now and forever to stay hidden.

If you are getting a new job that deposits checks, or want to keep your money safe without having to carry large amounts with you all the time, you must have some place to keep it. Banks must have certain information on depositors to stay within the legal parameters.

The US PATRIOT Act was brought into law in 2003 after the terrorist attacks of September 11, 2001 in an effort to know the identity by the banks of anyone trying to do business with them. The Customer Identification Program requires banks to know the name, date of birth, address, and Social Security Number or Passport number of any individual that opens an account with them. This will make it more difficult to stay under the radar if you have to give them these things.

One option that people have used is to set up an offshore bank account in a foreign country. This used to be reserved for people with large sums of money that wanted to hide money from the government's hands to tax it. This is available to the average Joe now as long as you do some research into the rules and laws regarding opening an account.

You can cash checks without a bank account. If you get a check, you can take it to the bank the check is written on and they will give you the funds. Another option is to go to large retailers such as Walmart that will cash a check as long as you are willing to pay the fee attached to getting money from them. Look around at different places in your area for the fees they charge you. Another option you have is to sign the check over to another person and have them give you the cash for it.

Another option to remain anonymous is by using a cryptocurrency such as Bitcoin. Many have a way for you to add cash anonymously and take money out anonymously at certain locations. You can stash as much cash as you want into the cryptocurrencies and other than the fees for the transactions, you will not have any other charges.

he values go up and down on these platforms, although they are a non-centralized digital currency so your privacy is tact. As they have only been in existence for about 10 years, many retailers are not accepting these as direct forms of ayments yet. The list of companies and the things you can purchase using cryptocurrency is growing each year and that end should continue. Check them out as an option for you.

o set up a bank account if you must, use a business as the name on the account because this will keep anyone from eing able to access your information and money. One guy had some bad debt and was ordered through the court to ave his bank account funds seized. His paycheck went into that account. He went to the bank and opened a business ccount and had his paycheck direct deposited into that account and the people trying to get his money couldn't ecause it was under the business name.

ry to use the bank account as little as possible and stay away from writing checks. Use the bank account only to get oney in if you must from employers or business payments, and take cash out to use or put on prepaid cards. You can so use it to fund cryptocurrencies if you choose to go that route. The less documented transactions you have, the more u stay under the radar.

you must use a bank, pick a small bank or credit union rather than a big national bank. If you can stay away from using bank at all, do so.

hen it comes to medical insurance and medical treatment you can be outed by the information you provide them. The est way to avoid giving them correct information is by paying cash for the things you need done. It is simple to find you ven if someone does not provide the medical facilities with their name. If you give your true date of birth and your true p code, you can easily be found. How many people in your zip code have your date of birth?

ist because you are under the radar does not mean that you stop paying taxes. This whole book was a guidebook to each you how to disappear from the radar and allow no one to find you. You must always file your taxes and you can do at without the government knowing where you really are living. If you have back taxes that you owe or have student ebt that has gone into arrears, your tax money will be taken while you are on the run.

earn to live without it and know that the government is getting at least some money from you to pay off the debt. hen you disappear and if you are in this type of situation it is best to try to pay these things on top of the taxes the overnment will take. Obviously do this anonymously.

you are running from other bad debt through loans or credit cards, it will eventually fall off your credit report and will away. As I said earlier, it can take up to 20 years and if it is a significant amount, the companies you owe will put uch resources into trying to find you. You must stay under the radar until this happens.

you are a criminal, many crimes have a statute of limitations. This means that after a period of time they will not be ile to bring you to justice for what you did. Some states though will pause that time of the statute of limitations for ome offenses if they know that you have run and are in hiding. Others extend the period for the statute of limitations or a set period if you run.

here are some crimes, all felony that some states have no statue of limitations. Some examples are murder, treason, exual crimes, and even embezzlement. Look up your state and Federal statues to see what you qualify for if you are inning from criminal activities. The type of crime and the statute will directly impact how deep under you must go and ow long you must stay hidden.

3

Final thoughts

As I started this conversation with you, many people think about the idea and possibility of starting a new life and having a fresh start. Few have the testicular fortitude to do it because they don't know what to do and are scared to try. If you are contemplating it, you can do it with the proper resources, planning, and time.

You have read through the book now and have a grasp on the magnitude of what you are getting ready to embark on. This will be a long, hard journey for those that are up for the challenge and if done right you will be more invisible than 95% of the people in America. Going under the radar and disappearing is something most people would not even really contemplate let alone do.

As stated early on in the book, the more time, effort, and planning you put into your disappearing the better your vanishing will be. Once you get to your new home too, planning and preparation to stay hidden and deep under takes a lot of work too. This will set you up long-term though and set you for life if you want to stay hidden forever. It will give you the chance to fix in yourself and your life the things that made you make the decision to take this journey.

It is a lonely journey in the beginning and it will take time to get back into socializing again, but it can be done. The reason you are doing this is because you are unhappy enough in your current situation that pressing reset and starting over is the best option you have come to.

I was born and raised into a middle-class life and the only dream I had as a child was to get a good job, the little house with a white picket fence, and to have an adoring wife and a couple of kids. My childhood did not prepare me for that because of my family and the situation I grew up in. I tried to push through that and make it happen anyway, and made many bad decisions along the way that seemed to overwhelm me and my life. Things didn't get better.

One day I thought to myself, I wonder if it were possible to walk away from my life and forget everything about it. Is it possible to leave and disappear from everyone and everything from my past life to just walk away? This led me on an exciting path and journey to my own discovery and it took many places to research and find the best way to legally escape it all and stay off the radar to everything and everyone in my past and start over again.

Through trials and experience, I put together a plan and put in the effort to make my own escape possible and look up the best ways to have my own experience. Once everything was gathered and in a big jumbled pile, I thought to myself that there are likely many more individuals that are researching information and want to make their own DOV. So, that is how this book came into being and laid the groundwork for all this information to be compiled for you.

This is the best information that I have at this point, and after writing the book it will probably lead to future renditions that include many more details of how to do the things outlined.

I will also be diving deeper into the how of many things in this book that will go into the next editions of the book. If you would like the updates without buying the book then send me an email with your name and put in the subject line "Email Updates" and they will be sent to you.

Until then, do not be afraid of what you are contemplating, this is an exciting journey that you are starting on and the outcomes are endless. I bid you farewell and wish you the best of luck... please send me an email (anonymously of course) to tell me your story and how you successfully disappeared. I would like to put up a website in the future with all the stories I compile.

Thanks,
Robert

Email me at: r.a.disappear@gmail.com

Printed in Great Britain
by Amazon